THE
MARINER'S
BOOK of DAYS

2017

Sheridan House

Sea Fever

by John Masefield

I must go down to the seas again, to the lonely sea and the sky,
And all I ask is a tall ship and a star to steer her by;
And the wheel's kick and the wind's song and the white sail's shaking,
And a grey mist on the sea's face, and a grey dawn breaking.

I must go down to the seas again, for the call of the running tide
Is a wild call and a clear call that may not be denied;
And all I ask is a windy day with the white clouds flying,
And the flung spray and the blown spume, and the sea-gulls crying.

I must go down to the seas again, to the vagrant gypsy life,
To the gull's way and the whale's way where the wind's like a whetted knife;
And all I ask is a merry yarn from a laughing fellow-rover,
And quiet sleep and a sweet dream when the long trick's over.

It is trite to say that our lives are subject to chance, but sometimes a humble pilot appears mysteriously and points a new course.
— Gershom Bradford, from *Yonder is the Sea*

The World's Oceans

Ocean	Area in sq. mi.	Avg. depth	Deepest pt.
Pacific	60,060,700	13,215 ft	36,198 ft
Atlantic	29,637,900	12,880 ft	30,246 ft
Indian	26,469,500	13,002 ft	24,460 ft
Southern	7,848,300	14,400 ft	23,736 ft
Arctic	5,427,000	3,953 ft	18,456 ft

The four-masted barque *Falls of Halladale* wrecked near Peterborough, Victoria, Australia 1908, photographer unknown.

For one thing, I was no longer alone; a
man is never alone with the wind—and
the boat made three.

—Hilaire Belloc

January

SUNDAY

1

New Year's Day

MONDAY

2

TUESDAY

3

WEDNESDAY

4

THURSDAY ◖

5

FRIDAY

6

SATURDAY

7

Racing yacht *Rawhiti,* a gaff-rigged cutter built in 1905 in Auckland, New Zealand, by the Logan Brothers for racing in Sydney Harbor.

Traditional Toasts of the British Royal Navy

Monday: Our ships at sea.

Tuesday: Our men.

Wednesday: Ourselves—as no one else is likely to concern themselves with our welfare.

Thursday: A bloody war and quick promotion.

Friday: A willing soul and sea room.

Saturday: Sweethearts and wives, may they never meet.

Sunday: Absent friends and those at sea.

But the standing toast that pleased the most was,

> The wind that blows
> The ship that goes
> And the lass that
> Loved a sailor!

The largest ocean current in the world is the Antarctic Circumpolar Current (ACC). The ACC flows west to east around Antarctica and is the dominant circulation engine in the Southern Ocean. It circulates through the Atlantic, Pacific, and Indian Oceans, and prevents warm water from reaching Antarctica. The ACC's strength is legendary and has always made the journey treacherous for vessels sailing east to west around Cape Horn.

It's out there at sea that you are really yourself.

—Vito Dumas

January

SUNDAY
8

MONDAY
9

TUESDAY
10

WEDNESDAY
11

THURSDAY   ○
12

FRIDAY
13

SATURDAY
14

January

SUNDAY

15

MONDAY

16

Martin Luther King Jr. Day

TUESDAY

17

WEDNESDAY

18

THURSDAY   ▶

19

FRIDAY

20

SATURDAY

21

Sailors, with their built-in sense of order. service, and discipline, should really be running the world.
—Nicholas Monsarrat

January

SUNDAY
22

MONDAY
23

TUESDAY
24

WEDNESDAY
25

THURSDAY
26

FRIDAY   ●
27

SATURDAY
28

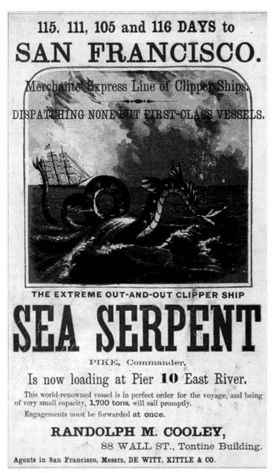

Sailing card for the clipper ship *Sea Serpent*, c. 1855.

The Sailor's Resolve

A sailor on the topsail yard,
　　While reefing softly sings,
"I'd rather pick some cherries here
　　Than pull on these 'ere strings.

"I'd sooner of a kicking mule
　　Be the undisputed boss,
Than haul this weather ear-ring out
　　On this 'ere Flemish hoss.

"I'd rather steer my Betsy Jane
　　Up to the alter rail,
Than be aloft on this 'ere night,
　　A reefin' this 'ere sail.

"I swear that when I get ashor
　　I'll splice that lovely lass,
Buy that aforesaid mule as kicks,
　　And peddle garden sass."

ALAS AND ALACK FOR HUMAN HOPES. Had a lively sou'west wind last evening, just where it should be, which promised to get us in within a few days, but in the night there blew up a raging nor'easter, chasing the sou'wester back to the Gulf and us off our course, and here we are somewhere between Greenwich and Hawaii, God knows where. Just tacked ship to get back on course for Nantucket but not doing too well close-hauled. Passed two six-masters southbound and a steamer, which shows we are in the right direction for Nantucket Lightship. Fred put his whole palm on the chart and said, "We're near here." Too overcast for sights, so we'll navigate "by guess and by God" until the sun pops out. Fred's hand covers nearly hundred miles radius.

— Dorothea Moulton Balano, from *The Log of the Skipper's Wife*

SUNDAY
29

MONDAY
30

TUESDAY
31

WEDNESDAY
1

THURSDAY
2

Groundhog Day

FRIDAY
3

◖

SATURDAY
4

February

It isn't that life ashore is distasteful to me. But life at sea is better.

—Sir Francis Drake

SUNDAY

5

MONDAY

6

TUESDAY

7

WEDNESDAY

8

THURSDAY

9

FRIDAY ○

10

SATURDAY

11

February

SUNDAY
12

MONDAY
13

TUESDAY
14

Valentine's Day

WEDNESDAY
15

THURSDAY
16

FRIDAY
17

SATURDAY ▸
18

WHEN BUT A MERE CHILD I used to fairly worship anything relating to the sea. Stories of adventure told by those who had seen the ocean and sailed on it filled me with awe. For hours at a time I used to sit on the town dock at Poughkeepsie, with the broad waters of the Hudson flowing past, and listen to the tales told by the congregation of boatmen who lounged about the freight house waiting for the day boat. The clumsy river sloops and schooners passing up or down the river became full-rigged ships in my imagination, and whenever one of them beating down with the tide happened to stand in toward where I sat on the dock, I'd rehearse all the expressions I had heard the boatmen use. "Porret yer hellum," "Vast ye lubber," or "Hard down yer hellum" were expressions I'd rip out in childish mimicry and when, to prevent wrecking his craft against the pier the helmsman threw the heavily loaded craft into the wind and she shot past, her bluff bows slapping the wake, forereaching into the wind with her grimy, patched sails giving out cannon-like reports as the canvas slapped in the wind and the sloop filled away on the other tack, to sidle down the river and dwindle to a toy under the high west bank, I'd score a victory over one more bloody pirate and tramp home covered with glory and long to be a man that I might go to sea.

— Charles G. Davis, from *Around Cape Horn*

"Believe me, my friend, there is nothing — *absolutely nothing* — *half so much worth doing as simply messing about in boats."*

— *Water Rat,* The Wind in the Willows *by Kenneth Grahame*

The *Elissa*, which has sailed for three centuries, sailing up the channel into Port Galveston, Texas. (U.S. Navy photo)

Men in a ship are always looking up, and
men ashore are usually looking down.
—John Masefield

February

SUNDAY
19

MONDAY
20

Presidents' Day

TUESDAY
21

WEDNESDAY
22

THURSDAY
23

FRIDAY
24

SATURDAY
25

February/March

A collision at sea can ruin your whole day.

—Thucydides

SUNDAY

26

●

MONDAY

27

TUESDAY

28

WEDNESDAY

1

Ash Wednesday

THURSDAY

2

FRIDAY

3

SATURDAY

4

*Without patience, a sailor I
would never be.*
—Lee Allred

March

SUNDAY

5

MONDAY

6

TUESDAY

7

WEDNESDAY

8

THURSDAY

9

FRIDAY

10

SATURDAY

11

A "12 pounder" carronade on a 19th-century brig of war.

Provisioning an Ocean Liner

For a single transatlantic voyage, the RMS Oceanic *(White Star line 1899–1914) was laden with the following provisions:*

200 barrels (17.5 tons) of flour

50,000 lbs of beef and mutton

12,000 lbs of lamb, pork, and veal

8,000 lbs of poultry and game

4,000 lbs of smoked meats

5,000 lbs of butter

2,000 eggs

3,000 quarts of milk

3,000 quarts of ice cream

10,000 lbs of sugar

2,500 lbs of oatmeal

3,000 lbs of rice

46 tons of potatoes

Random tons of other fruit and vegetables

Also beer, enough for a gallon a day for the men, and rum, arak, brandy, and claret

WE HAD DULL, RAINY WEATHER in the former part of our voyage and came near encountering a water spout. The wind was light at the time and the weather thick and rainy; the spout was slowly approaching us. We made every effort in our power to avoid it, but probably should have failed to do so but for the circumstance of its breaking when within about a hundred rods of us and falling with a mighty splash to the surface.

This phenomenon has a very singular appearance when near to it; the water is in a wild state of agitation for a large circle about its base and appears to move in a circular direction. The spout, which looks very black, extends from the surface of the ocean to the cloud into which the water appears to enter, and is so much larger at the base than at the cloud and, though appearing to move in a circular direction, moves with considerable speed in a right line, and when near them the water is plainly to be seen ascending to the cloud.

— Capt. Theodore Wells, from *Narrative of the Life and Adventures of Capt. Theodore Wells*

. . . And all I ask for is sunshine and a good sailing breeze.
—Richard Baum

March

SUNDAY

12

○

Daylight Saving Time begins

MONDAY

13

TUESDAY

14

WEDNESDAY

15

THURSDAY

16

FRIDAY

17

St. Patrick's Day

SATURDAY

18

March

SUNDAY

19

MONDAY

20

Vernal Equinox

TUESDAY

21

WEDNESDAY

22

THURSDAY

23

FRIDAY

24

SATURDAY

25

Out of sight of land the sailor feels safe.
It is the beach that worries him.
—Charles G. Davis

March / April

SUNDAY
26

MONDAY ●
27

TUESDAY
28

WEDNESDAY
29

THURSDAY
30

FRIDAY
31

SATURDAY
1

April Fool's Day

Most ships' wheels are on the starboard side because it provides a better view of vessels approaching from the starboard, to which you must give way. It is also a holdover from the turn of the twentieth century, when more and more ships were becoming motorized. When moving at high speeds, the torque from the prop caused long, narrow vessels to lift their starboard sides. So all extra weight, including the helmsman, was placed on the starboard side to keep the boat level.

The two-sail bateau *E. C. Collier* under sail, dredging oysters in Chesapeake Bay. Photographer and date unknown. (Chesapeake Bay Maritime Museum, St. Michaels, Maryland)

Any fool can carry on, but only the wise man knows how to shorten sail.

—Joseph Conrad

April

SUNDAY

2

MONDAY

◖

3

TUESDAY

4

WEDNESDAY

5

THURSDAY

6

FRIDAY

7

SATURDAY

8

April

SUNDAY

9

Palm Sunday

MONDAY

10

Passover begins

TUESDAY

11

○

WEDNESDAY

12

THURSDAY

13

FRIDAY

14

Good Friday

SATURDAY

15

The sea finds out everything you did wrong.
—Francis Stokes

April

SUNDAY

16

Easter

MONDAY

17

Patriot's Day

TUESDAY

18

Passover ends

WEDNESDAY ◗

19

THURSDAY

20

FRIDAY

21

SATURDAY

22

Earth Day

The merchant vessel *Mary Celeste* under sail, ca. 1861. Artist unknown.

The *Mary Celeste* was an American brigantine that was found drifting off the Azores on December 4, 1872. She was in seaworthy condition, under partial sail, but there was no one aboard, and her lifeboat was gone. The last log entry was from ten days prior.

She had sailed from New York City on November 7, still had ample provisions, and her cargo of denatured alcohol was intact. Stranger still, the personal effects of the captain and crew were undisturbed. Of those who had been on board—the captain, his wife, their two-year-old daughter, and the crew of seven—none were ever seen or heard from again.

The mystery of just what caused a crew to abandon a perfectly seaworthy vessel has never been answered, though numerous theories have been put forth, including undersea earthquakes, giant squid, waterspouts, a bizarre reaction of the crew to alcohol fumes from the cargo, and even a paranormal occurrence.

Knot Knowledge

Generally considered to be the best all-around knot, the bowline (bo-lin) is easy to tie and untie, tightens as tension is applied, and never jams.

However, every time you turn, loop, or twist a line to tie a knot you also reduce the rope's strength. A bowline can reduce the strength of a line by up to 40 percent.

The best knot for maintaining line strength: the anchor bend, which reduces a rope's strength by only 24 percent.

Cruising has two pleasures. One is to go out in
wider waters from a sheltered place. The other is
to go into a sheltered place from wider waters.
—Howard Bloomfield

April

SUNDAY
23

MONDAY
24

TUESDAY
25

WEDNESDAY   ●
26

THURSDAY
27

FRIDAY
28

SATURDAY
29

April / May

SUNDAY
30

MONDAY
1

TUESDAY
2

◖

WEDNESDAY
3

THURSDAY
4

FRIDAY
5

Cinco de Mayo

SATURDAY
6

I start from the premise that no object created by man is as satisfying to his body and soul as a proper sailing yacht.

—Arthur Beiser

May

SUNDAY

7

MONDAY

8

TUESDAY

9

WEDNESDAY   ○

10

THURSDAY

11

FRIDAY

12

SATURDAY

13

Bluenose pulls away, 1921. Photographer unknown.

Bluenose was a Canadian schooner built in Nova Scotia in 1921. A celebrated racing and fishing vessel under the command of Angus Waters, in the 1930s she became an important cultural icon of Nova Scotia and Canada. She was even honored with a postage stamp.

What's in Your Ditty Bag

A ditty bag is a small canvas sack with a drawstring in which mariners for centuries have carried their gear for sail and rope repair.

Sailmaker's needles

Palm: *A heavy pad for pushing needles through sailcloth or rope.*

Thread

Beeswax

Fid: *Used for splicing rope, a fid is an 8-inch wooden taper that opens a gap between strands without harming the individual fibers.*

Marlinspike: *Like a fid, except made of metal and used for splicing wire.*

Butane lighter: *Used to heat-seal the end of a line.*

Lanolin

½-inch masking tape

Needle-nose pliers

Scraps of sailcloth

2-inch sail repair tape

Monel wire: *For seizing shackle pins in position.*

I wanted freedom, open air, adventure.
I found it on the sea.
                —Alain Gerbault

May

SUNDAY
14

Mother's Day

MONDAY
15

TUESDAY
16

WEDNESDAY
17

THURSDAY   ▶
18

FRIDAY
19

SATURDAY
20

May

The goal is not to sail the boat, but
rather to help the boat sail herself.
—John Rousmaniere

SUNDAY
21

MONDAY
22

TUESDAY
23

WEDNESDAY
24

THURSDAY ●
25

FRIDAY
26

SATURDAY
27

Ramadan begins

There are only two colors to paint a boat, black or white, and only a fool would paint a boat black.

—Nathanael Herreshoff

SUNDAY

28

MONDAY

29

Memorial Day

TUESDAY

30

WEDNESDAY

31

THURSDAY

1

◖

FRIDAY

2

SATURDAY

3

A squadron of the Royal Navy running down the channel and an East Indiaman preparing to sail. Samual Atkins, date unknown.

Hull Down t' Le'ward

Across the restless heaving sea,
  Neath the scud, with gale a-pulling,
Every twanging shroud and spar,
  Swift the wind ships canvas piling,
Gathering fragrant spoil afar;
  Daring masters and the misters,
Are but mem'ries, damned or shriven,
  Round foc'sl stoves in canisters,
Enwrapped in steel, pow'r driven.

The Neptune Oath
(to make a sailor of David Robinson)

"You, David Robinson, will never row when you can sail, will never walk when you can ride, will never kiss the maid when you can the mistress. When you are boarded by Neptune and he wants to know if you are one of his subjects, you tell him you took the oath off Parker's Flats in 1828, administered by Skipper Davis."

— Capt. John Pendleton Farrow, from *The Romantic Story of David Robertson*

SUNDAY

4

MONDAY

5

TUESDAY

6

WEDNESDAY

7

THURSDAY

8

FRIDAY

9

○

SATURDAY

10

June

SUNDAY

11

MONDAY

12

TUESDAY

13

WEDNESDAY

14

Flag Day

THURSDAY

15

FRIDAY

16

SATURDAY

17

To touch that bow is to rest one's hands
on the cosmic nose of things.
—Jack London

June

SUNDAY
18

Father's Day

MONDAY
19

TUESDAY
20

WEDNESDAY
21

Summer Solstice

THURSDAY
22

FRIDAY
23

●

SATURDAY
24

I HEARD THE CAPTAIN TELL THE MATE TO SEND A MAN aloft to reef the pendant halyards. After making several efforts, the man came down and reported that it would be impossible without launching the top-gallant mast. Three others went up and all of them brought the same report. I was still at the helm, and felt my ambition excited. I called to an old Scotchman to relieve the helm, then went up to the head of the top-gallant rigging and took a look at the situation, and secretly regretted having left the helm. We were sailing by the wind, under single-reefed topsails, and the brig rolled considerably, which was much more perceivable aloft than on deck.

It was greasy and very slippery. I made the attempt and at every effort gained a little, until I could throw my hand over the truck, holding the end of the halyards in my teeth, and having gained this much I urged myself up higher and accomplished my purpose. I then slid down to the head of the rigging and stopped to take breath, and felt convinced that I had more courage than discretion.

— Capt. Theodore Wells, from *Narrative of the Life and Adventures of Capt. Theodore Wells*

Illustration of the first American sea serpent, reported from Cape Ann, Massachusetts, in 1639. Illustrator unknown.

Rule of Thumb

According to lore, the phrase "rule of thumb" originated with old-time ship captains, who used the width of their thumb on a chart to steer clear of obstacles.

In 1801, the U.S. Navy consisted of the following ships:

United States	*44 guns*
President	*44*
Constitution	*44*
Philadelphia	*44*
Chesapeake	*36*
Constellation	*36*
Congress	*36*
New York	*36*
Boston	*32*
Essex	*32*
Adams	*32*
John Adams	*32*
General Greene	*32*

In 1790, a law had been passed calling for six ships of 74 guns each to be built, but the law was never put into effect.

At sea, I learned how little a person needs, not how much.
　　　　　　　　　—Robin Lee Graham

June / July

SUNDAY
25

Ramadan ends

MONDAY
26

TUESDAY
27

WEDNESDAY
28

THURSDAY
29

FRIDAY
30

◖

SATURDAY
1

July

SUNDAY

2

MONDAY

3

TUESDAY

4

Independence Day

WEDNESDAY

5

THURSDAY

6

FRIDAY

7

SATURDAY

8

There is pleasure unknown to the landsman in reading at sea.
—William McFee

July

SUNDAY ○

9

MONDAY

10

TUESDAY

11

WEDNESDAY

12

THURSDAY

13

FRIDAY

14

SATURDAY

15

The USS *Constitution* fires a 21-gun salute during the ship's annual under way in Boston Harbor on July 4, 2011. First launched in 1797, *Constitution* was one of six ships ordered for construction by President George Washington to protect America's maritime interests. She is the oldest commissioned warship afloat in the world. (U.S. Navy photo)

On the Origin of SOS

Contrary to popular lore, the distress signal SOS has nothing to do with "Save Our Ship," "Save Our Souls," or any other acronym. The 1908 international agreement settled on three dots, three dashes, three dots as the universal signal for distress because the pattern was easy to memorize. It is mere coincidence that it spells SOS.

The USS *Hornet* and the *Peacock*

Captain Lawrence immediately ordered his men to quarters, and had the ship cleared for action. He kept close by the wind, in order, if possible, to get the weathergage of the approaching vessel. Finding he could weather the enemy, he hoisted American colors and tacked. About a quarter of an hour after this, the ships passed each other, and exchannged broadsides within half pistol shot. Captain Lawrence, observing the enemy in the act of wearing, bore up, received his starboard broadside, and ran him close on board on the starboard quarter. From that position he kept up a most severe and well directed fire. So great was its effect, that, in less than fifteen minutes the British vessel struck. She was almost cut to pieces, and hoisted an ensign, union down, from her fore rigging as a signal of distress.

— from *The Naval Battles of the United States*, 1857

Being hove to in a long gale is the most
boring way of being terrified I know.
—Donald Hamilton

July

SUNDAY

16

MONDAY

17

TUESDAY

18

WEDNESDAY

19

THURSDAY

20

FRIDAY

21

SATURDAY

22

July

SUNDAY ●

23

MONDAY

24

TUESDAY

25

WEDNESDAY

26

THURSDAY

27

FRIDAY

28

SATURDAY

29

The man who has experienced shipwreck
shudders even at a calm sea.

— Ovid

July / August

SUNDAY

30

MONDAY

31

TUESDAY

1

WEDNESDAY

2

THURSDAY

3

FRIDAY

4

SATURDAY

5

Illustration of the HMS *Endymion* rounding the Horn, by Herbert Roxby, from aboard the HMS *Liverpool*, 1871.

I REALLY DON'T KNOW WHY it is that all of us are so committed to the sea, except I think it's because in addition to the fact that the sea changes, and the light changes, and ships change, it's because we all came from the sea. And it is an interesting biological fact that all of us have in our veins the exact same percentage of salt in our blood that exists in the ocean, and, therefore, we have salt in our blood, in our sweat, in our tears. We are tied to the ocean. And when we go back to the sea—whether it is to sail or to watch it—we are going back from whence we came.

—John F. Kennedy, remarks at the Dinner for the America's Cup Crews, September 14 1962

Some Mighty Big Ships

The biggest ship ever built was the super-tanker Knock Nevis, *which was 253 feet longer than the height of the Empire State Building. The largest schooner—and the only seven-masted schooner—ever built was the steel-hulled* Thomas W. Lawson (below).

HMS Victory, *1765, 226.5 ft, 2,162 tons*

Thos. W. Lawson, *1902, 475 ft, 5,218 tons*

RMS Titanic, *1911, 882.5 ft, 46,328 tons*

Bismarck, *1939, 823 ft, 44,734 tons*

USS Enterprise, *1961, 1,123 ft, 89,600 tons*

RMS Queen Mary 2, *1,132 ft, 150,000 tons*

Knock Nevis, *1979, 1,504 ft, 260,941 tons*

The fishermen know that the sea is dangerous and the storm terrible, but they have never found these dangers sufficient reason for remaining ashore.

—Vincent Van Gogh

August

SUNDAY

6

MONDAY   ○

7

TUESDAY

8

WEDNESDAY

9

THURSDAY

10

FRIDAY

11

SATURDAY

12

August

SUNDAY

13

MONDAY

▶

14

TUESDAY

15

WEDNESDAY

16

THURSDAY

17

FRIDAY

18

SATURDAY

19

The pessimist complains about the wind;
the optimist expects it to change; the realist
adjusts the sails.
  —William Arthur Ward

August

SUNDAY
20

MONDAY   ●
21

TUESDAY
22

WEDNESDAY
23

THURSDAY
24

FRIDAY
25

SATURDAY
26

Why Rum?

Since the earliest days of sail, fresh water would not keep for long on board ship. At first wine or beer was substituted, then brandy was in use in the mid-1600s. Once Jamaica was conquered, rum became the favored drink because it was cheap and easy to make.

As raw sugar was cured, molasses would drain out. This was allowed to naturally ferment, then it was distilled into a clear liquid, which gradually darkened as it aged in wooden barrels.

The English called it *rum-bullion*, later shortened to rum, perhaps because it seemed *rum* (odd) to get something valuable (*bullion*) from what was essentially trash.

Do they ask me what pleasure I find on the sea?
— Why, absence from land is a pleasure to me:
A hamper of porter, and plenty of grog,
A friend, when too sleepy, to give me a jog,
A coop that will always some poultry afford,
Some bottles of gin, and no parson on board,
A crew that is brisk when it happens to blow,
One compass on deck and another below,
A girl, with more sense than the girl at the head,
To read me a novel, or make up me bed —
The man that has these, has a treasure in store
That millions possess not who live upon shore.

— Philip Freneau

Mutiny at sea, from the book, *A Sailor in Spite of Himself,* by Harry Castlemon, 1898.

Never before have I experi-
enced such beauty and fear
at the same time.
—Ellen MacArthur

August/September

SUNDAY

27

MONDAY

28

TUESDAY

29

WEDNESDAY

30

THURSDAY

31

FRIDAY

1

SATURDAY

2

September

SUNDAY

3

MONDAY

4

Labor Day

TUESDAY

5

WEDNESDAY ○

6

THURSDAY

7

FRIDAY

8

SATURDAY

9

The wind and the waves are always on
the side of the ablest navigator.
—Edward Gibbon

September

SUNDAY

10

MONDAY

11

Patriot Day

TUESDAY

12

WEDNESDAY ▶

13

THURSDAY

14

FRIDAY

15

SATURDAY

16

The engagement between the British sloop-of-war *Drake* and the Continental Navy vessel *Ranger*, commanded by John Paul Jones, 1778. Artist unknown.

Qualifications of a Naval Officer

It is by no means enough that an officer of the navy should be a capable mariner. He must be that, of course, but also a great deal more. He should be as well a gentleman of liberal education, refined manners, punctilious courtesy, and the nicest sense of personal honor. He should be the soul of tact, patience, justice, firmness, and charity. No meritorious act of a subordinate should escape his attention or be left to pass without its reward, even if the reward is only a word of approval. Conversely, he should not be blind to a single fault in any subordinate, though, at the same time, he should be quick and unfailing to distinguish error from malice, thoughtlessness from incompetency, and well meant shortcoming from heedless or stupid blunder.

— John Paul Jones

Many animals, such as hares, pigs, and black cats, could not be carried or mentioned on ship board except under stringent conditions. Often a pig was carried in a crate to eat the slops, but this animal was foredoomed for execution at some point to provide fresh meat and therefore did not come under ban. Every black cat was supposed to carry a gale in her tail and if she frolicked a storm was sure to come.

— *Edmund Ogden Sawyer Jr., from* Our Sea Saga

Sailing is just the bottom line, like
adding up the score in bridge. My real
interest is in the tremendous game of life.
—Dennis Conner

September

SUNDAY
17

MONDAY
18

TUESDAY
19

WEDNESDAY ●
20

Rosh Hashanah

THURSDAY
21

FRIDAY
22

Autumnal Equinox

SATURDAY
23

September

There are three sorts of people; those who are alive, those who are dead, and those who are at sea.

—Anacharsis

SUNDAY

24

MONDAY

25

TUESDAY

26

WEDNESDAY   ☾

27

THURSDAY

28

FRIDAY

29

Yom Kippur

SATURDAY

30

He that will not sail till all dangers are
over must never put to sea.
—Thomas Fuller

October

SUNDAY

1

MONDAY

2

TUESDAY

3

WEDNESDAY

4

THURSDAY   ○

5

FRIDAY

6

SATURDAY

7

A TRADEWIND STARTS GENTLY, without gusts—a huge ocean of air that slowly and resolutely begins to move with ever-increasing strength. Suddenly everything comes to life. Spirits rise as the sails fill. The boat heels slightly and moves ahead. The almost oppressive silence gives way to the sound of the bow cutting through the water. Gone is the sea's glassy surface, and with it the terrible glare. Close the hatches and ports! We're sailing again!

— Jim Moore, from *By Way of the Wind*

"City Ice Boat No. 3," by George Essig, 1877. The painting depicts Philadelphia's City Ice Boat No. 3 towing a sailing ship with a damaged mast through ice floes on the Delaware River.

A wondrous tale, could the rare old whale
Of the mighty deep disclose;
Of the skeleton forms, of by-gone storms,
And of treasures, that no one knows.

He has seen the crew, when the tempest blew
Drop down from the slippery Deck,
As he shook the tide, from his glassy side,
And sporting 'mongst Ocean and wreck.

— *George Blanchard, from his 1847 journal*

THE MEN WHO SPENT THE better part of three to four years on isolated waters, contending with ennui or overwork, relaxed contentment or desparate exhaustion, brought much more to their endeavors than their capable hands, willing energy, and their sense of humor or outrage. They came whaling with ambition and interest and endowed their experience with distinctive meaning. Most seaman claimed that surviving the whale hunt enhanced their manhood.

— Margaret S. Creighton, from *Rites & Passages, The Experience of American Whaling, 1830–1870*

Sailing: the fine art of slowly going nowhere at great expense while being cold, wet, and miserable.

—Irv Heller

October

SUNDAY

8

MONDAY

9

Columbus Day

TUESDAY

10

WEDNESDAY

11

THURSDAY ▶

12

FRIDAY

13

SATURDAY

14

October

SUNDAY
15

MONDAY
16

TUESDAY
17

WEDNESDAY
18

THURSDAY ●
19

FRIDAY
20

SATURDAY
21

I'm telling you that India is that way, now set my course.
—Christopher Columbus

October

SUNDAY

22

MONDAY

23

TUESDAY

24

WEDNESDAY

25

THURSDAY

26

FRIDAY

27

◖

SATURDAY

28

The *Imperator Alexander* running before a heavy gale, 1885, photographer unknown.

Waves are not measured in feet or inches, they are measured in increments of fear.

— *Buzzy Trent*

Rogue Waves

Rogue, or freak, waves seem to occur at random. For centuries there have been stories of hundred-foot-tall walls of water appearing without warning. The waves often occurred in clear weather and against the current, but were not considered scientifically valid until 1995. Current evidence shows that they are more common than previously thought, yet it is still not known just what causes them.

1933: The USS *Ramapo* was struck by a 112-foot wave in the North Pacific

1942: The RMS *Queen Mary,* carrying 15,000 American troops, was hit by a 92-foot wave and listed 52 degrees before righting.

1966: The Italian liner *Michelangelo* lost a crewman and two passengers when a wave broke a hole in the suprestructure 80 feet above the waterline.

1995: The *Queen Elizabeth 2* was hit by a 95-foot wave. which her captain said, "looked like the white cliffs of dover."

2005: *Norwegian Dawn* was hit by a three 70-foot waves in a row.

October/November

SUNDAY

29

MONDAY

30

TUESDAY

31

Halloween

WEDNESDAY

1

THURSDAY

2

FRIDAY

3

SATURDAY ○

4

November

SUNDAY

5

Daylight Saving Time ends

MONDAY

6

TUESDAY

7

Election Day

WEDNESDAY

8

THURSDAY

9

FRIDAY

10

◗

SATURDAY

11

Veterans Day

Off Cape Horn there are but two kinds of
weather, neither one of them a pleasant kind.
—John Masefield

November

SUNDAY
12

MONDAY
13

TUESDAY
14

WEDNESDAY
15

THURSDAY
16

FRIDAY
17

SATURDAY ●
18

Sailing Philosophy of the U.S. Naval Academy

We teach sailing and seamanship at the naval academy for one purpose: to make competent seamen of our midshipmen, who will be the naval leaders of the future. We aren't interested in making yachtsmen of them. We enter races to find an atmosphere which, like combat, stretches ability and endurance to the limit and allows character to emerge that can reach beyond those previous limits for that extra margin required for victory, where decisions must be made instantly and be coupled with competent execution of complex evolutions. Where numerous variables must be integrated to derive tactics and strategy in interaction. And we send them to sea to learn the fundamental characteristic of the professional seaman: a deep-seated sense of humility in the face of nature and her master. But we never lose sight of our objective—to produce the best possible officer for the fleet, whether he or she is assigned to a surface ship, a submarine, or an aircraft.

— Captain J. B. Bonds, USN

Green Around the Gills

or some salty terms for throwing up due to seasickness

Blow chowder
Chum the waters
Drain the dinghy
Feed the fish
Splash the hash
Toss your tacos
Visible burp
Reverse gears
Launch lunch
Holler at the ocean
Stomach tsunami
Throat torpedoes
Paint the deck

Illustration of St. Elmo's fire on the masts of a ship, ca. 1866, artist unknown.

Borders? I have never seen one. But I have heard they exist in the minds of some people.

—Thor Heyerdahl

November

SUNDAY
19

MONDAY
20

TUESDAY
21

WEDNESDAY
22

THURSDAY
23

Thanksgiving

FRIDAY
24

SATURDAY
25

November/December

SUNDAY

26

MONDAY

27

TUESDAY

28

WEDNESDAY

29

THURSDAY

30

FRIDAY

1

SATURDAY

2

Ships are the nearest things to dreams
that hands have ever made.
—Robert N. Rose

December

SUNDAY

3

MONDAY

4

TUESDAY

5

WEDNESDAY

6

THURSDAY

7

Pearl Harbor Remembrance Day

FRIDAY

8

SATURDAY

9

A Gloucester fishing schooner at anchor on George's Bank. The crew is hand-lining cod and the vessel is rigged for rough weather. Paul E. Collins, date unknown.

THE SEA SEEMS TO BE THE great mother of all life . . . the vast expanse of water swarms everywhere with life in a hundred thousand forms. These forms lie or creep along the bottom and in its lowest depths; they float and swim in its currents; they rise and fall with its tides; they fringe its shores; and, in the extreme northern and southern regions, where the cold seems to render impossible even the temporary presence of man, this life thrives and multiplies in its most minute and most prodigious forms, and in as great an exuberance as it anywhere attains.

— Jacob Abbott, from *Water & Land*, Science for the Young, vol. III

Wadham's Song

From Bonavista to the Cabot Isles
The course is north full 40 miles
When you must steer away nor'east
Till Cape Freals, Gull Isle, bears
      west-nor'west
Then nor'-nor'west 33 miles
Three leagues offshore lies Wadham's
      Isles
Where of a rock you must be beware
Two miles sou'-sou'east from off
      isle bear.

—"Wadham's Song" is an example of a pilot verse, navigational directions sung to a popular song to help seamen memorize them.

One cannot look at the sea without
wishing for the wings of a swallow.
—Sir Richard Burton

December

SUNDAY
10

MONDAY
11

TUESDAY
12

Hanukkah begins

WEDNESDAY
13

THURSDAY
14

FRIDAY
15

SATURDAY
16

December

No matter how important a man at sea may consider himself, unless he is fundamentally worthy the sea will someday find him out.

—Felix Riesenberg

SUNDAY

17

MONDAY

18

●

TUESDAY

19

WEDNESDAY

20

THURSDAY

21

Winter Solstice

FRIDAY

22

SATURDAY

23

It was a strange and pleasant life for me all summer, sailing entirely alone by sea and river.

—John MacGregor

December

SUNDAY

24

MONDAY

25

Christmas Day

TUESDAY

26

◖

Kwanzaa begins

WEDNESDAY

27

THURSDAY

28

FRIDAY

29

SATURDAY

30

THE CLIPPER *TORNADO* ARRIVED in New York in 1852 with the foremast very nearly prostrate and the bowsprit broken off— the effect of a whilrwind in the Pacific a thousand miles west of Cape Horn. She had sailed in this condition 8,000 miles in sixty-five days.

"The shock," says the captain's log-book, "was instantaneous. The bowsprit was broken off close to the knight-heads, and the whole of it carried inboard on the port side. The foremast instantly followed it close to the deck, being lifted from between the main-stays so that the heel of it grazed the house, and went over the side tearing away the main and monkey rails. This immense weight of mast, yards, sails, and rigging lying across the main-stays had to be cut adrift to save the mainmast, which on examination was found to be sprung."

— Edmund Ogden Sawyer Jr., from *Our Sea Saga*

The origin of "Mind Your P's and Q's"

When sailors were ashore, they were given credit for their drinks at taverns. Beer was sold in pints and quarts, so the tab was tallied in columns labeled P and Q.

Unscrupulous barkeeps often took advantage of drunken sailors and added extra drinks to the tab. So sailors were always warned to keep accurate count of how many p's and q's they'd had to drink.

Sail and steam meet on the high seas, Hans Petersen, 1898.

No one likes an ugly boat, however cheap or fast.

—Roger Duncan

December/January

SUNDAY

31

MONDAY

1

New Year's Day

TUESDAY

2

WEDNESDAY

3

THURSDAY ○

4

FRIDAY

5

SATURDAY

6

Looking Astern
2017 at a glance

JANUARY

S	M	T	W	T	F	S
1	2	3	4	5	6	7
8	9	10	11	12	13	14
15	16	17	18	19	20	21
22	23	24	25	26	27	28
29	30	31				

FEBRUARY

S	M	T	W	T	F	S
			1	2	3	4
5	6	7	8	9	10	11
12	13	14	15	16	17	18
19	20	21	22	23	24	25
26	27	28				

MARCH

S	M	T	W	T	F	S
			1	2	3	4
5	6	7	8	9	10	11
12	13	14	15	16	17	18
19	20	21	22	23	24	25
26	27	28	29	30	31	

APRIL

S	M	T	W	T	F	S
						1
2	3	4	5	6	7	8
9	10	11	12	13	14	15
16	17	18	19	20	21	22
23	24	25	26	27	28	29
30						

MAY

S	M	T	W	T	F	S
	1	2	3	4	5	6
7	8	9	10	11	12	13
14	15	16	17	18	19	20
21	22	23	24	25	26	27
28	29	30	31			

JUNE

S	M	T	W	T	F	S
				1	2	3
4	5	6	7	8	9	10
11	12	13	14	15	16	17
18	19	20	21	22	23	24
25	26	27	28	29	30	

JULY

S	M	T	W	T	F	S
						1
2	3	4	5	6	7	8
9	10	11	12	13	14	15
16	17	18	19	20	21	22
23	24	25	26	27	28	29
30	31					

AUGUST

S	M	T	W	T	F	S
		1	2	3	4	5
6	7	8	9	10	11	12
13	14	15	16	17	18	19
20	21	22	23	24	25	26
27	28	29	30	31		

SEPTEMBER

S	M	T	W	T	F	S
					1	2
3	4	5	6	7	8	9
10	11	12	13	14	15	16
17	18	19	20	21	22	23
24	25	26	27	28	29	30

OCTOBER

S	M	T	W	T	F	S
1	2	3	4	5	6	7
8	9	10	11	12	13	14
15	16	17	18	19	20	21
22	23	24	25	26	27	28
29	30	31				

NOVEMBER

S	M	T	W	T	F	S
			1	2	3	4
5	6	7	8	9	10	11
12	13	14	15	16	17	18
19	20	21	22	23	24	25
26	27	28	29	30		

DECEMBER

S	M	T	W	T	F	S
					1	2
3	4	5	6	7	8	9
10	11	12	13	14	15	16
17	18	19	20	21	22	23
24	25	26	27	28	29	30
31						

Looking Ahead
2018 at a glance

JANUARY

S	M	T	W	T	F	S
	1	2	3	4	5	6
7	8	9	10	11	12	13
14	15	16	17	18	19	20
21	22	23	24	25	26	27
28	29	30	31			

FEBRUARY

S	M	T	W	T	F	S
				1	2	3
4	5	6	7	8	9	10
11	12	13	14	15	16	17
18	19	20	21	22	23	24
25	26	27	28			

MARCH

S	M	T	W	T	F	S
				1	2	3
4	5	6	7	8	9	10
11	12	13	14	15	16	17
18	19	20	21	22	23	24
25	26	27	28	29	30	31

APRIL

S	M	T	W	T	F	S
1	2	3	4	5	6	7
8	9	10	11	12	13	14
15	16	17	18	19	20	21
22	23	24	25	26	27	28
29	30					

MAY

S	M	T	W	T	F	S
		1	2	3	4	5
6	7	8	9	10	11	12
13	14	15	16	17	18	19
20	21	22	23	24	25	26
27	28	29	30	31		

JUNE

S	M	T	W	T	F	S
					1	2
3	4	5	6	7	8	9
10	11	12	13	14	15	16
17	18	19	20	21	22	23
24	25	26	27	28	29	30

JULY

S	M	T	W	T	F	S
1	2	3	4	5	6	7
8	9	10	11	12	13	14
15	16	17	18	19	20	21
22	23	24	25	26	27	28
29	30	31				

AUGUST

S	M	T	W	T	F	S
			1	2	3	4
5	6	7	8	9	10	11
12	13	14	15	16	17	18
19	20	21	22	23	24	25
26	27	28	29	30	31	

SEPTEMBER

S	M	T	W	T	F	S
						1
2	3	4	5	6	7	8
9	10	11	12	13	14	15
16	17	18	19	20	21	22
23	24	25	26	27	28	29
30						

OCTOBER

S	M	T	W	T	F	S
	1	2	3	4	5	6
7	8	9	10	11	12	13
14	15	16	17	18	19	20
21	22	23	24	25	26	27
28	29	30	31			

NOVEMBER

S	M	T	W	T	F	S
				1	2	3
4	5	6	7	8	9	10
11	12	13	14	15	16	17
18	19	20	21	22	23	24
25	26	27	28	29	30	

DECEMBER

S	M	T	W	T	F	S
						1
2	3	4	5	6	7	8
9	10	11	12	13	14	15
16	17	18	19	20	21	22
23	24	25	26	27	28	29
30	31					

Published by Sheridan House
An imprint of Globe Pequot
Trade division of The Rowman & Littlefield Publishing Group, Inc.
4501 Forbes Boulevard, Suite 200, Lanham, Maryland 20706
www.rowman.com

Unit A, Whitacre Mews, 26-34 Stannary Street, London SE11 4AB, United Kingdom

Distributed by NATIONAL BOOK NETWORK

ISBN 978-1-60893-473-7 (paperback : alk. paper)

☉™ The paper used in this publication meets the minimum requirements of American National Standard for Information Sciences—Permanence of Paper for Printed Library Materials, ANSI/NISO Z39.48-1992.

Printed in the United States of America